Original title:
Infinite Jest in Zero-G

Copyright © 2025 Creative Arts Management OÜ
All rights reserved.

Author: Alexander Thornton
ISBN HARDBACK: 978-1-80567-854-0
ISBN PAPERBACK: 978-1-80567-975-2

Cosmic Frolics

In a vacuum, giggles drift,
Asteroids prance, they play and shift.
Floating snacks in zero G,
We laugh so hard, we can't quite see.

Comets chase, they slip and slide,
With quirky friends, we take a ride.
Galactic jesters, full of glee,
In cosmic space, we're wild and free.

Light-Hearted in the Abyss

Gravity? Ha! Who needs that weight?
We're bouncing round, it's quite a fate.
Giant moons do waltzes, oh so grand,
   As we spin tales in wonderland.

Stars chuckle softly in the dark,
While nebulae flicker, leaving a mark.
The universe serves jokes and cheer,
   In this dark void, we hold it dear.

Asteroids of Amusement

Asteroids dance in chaotic bliss,
Meteors zoom with a wink and a hiss.
Cosmic pranks and celestial games,
In this weird realm, nothing's the same.

Space debris giggles in the breeze,
While planets twirl with effortless ease.
Each twist and turn brings delight,
As the universe shines, ever so bright.

Interstellar Play

Wormholes laugh as we peek inside,
Where time and space both shift and glide.
Playing tag with a starry glare,
The universe grins, we stop and stare.

Galaxies swirl in laughter and song,
Floating along where the stars belong.
In this big playground, freely we soar,
As laughter echoes, forevermore.

Uplifted Mirth

In a realm where giggles soar,
Gravitational pull is no more.
Floating jokes drift through the air,
Tickles land without a care.

Zero gravity, silly flight,
Punchlines bounce left and right.
Laughter leaps, a joyous spree,
In the vastness, wild and free.

Loops of Laughter

Round and round, the clown does spin,
In the void, where doeps begin.
Silly faces, rubber bands,
Orbiting jokes like merry bands.

Gravity's gone, so take a trip,
Jokes take off, they see a blip.
Cannonball laughter, zeroing in,
Floating high on a whimsy din.

Beyond the Atmosphere

Drifting past the stratosphere,
Punchlines rise without a fear.
Tickled fancies, spheres collide,
In this space where jesters glide.

Galaxies of giggles bloom,
Stars chuckle in the silent gloom.
Astro-funnies, a cosmic cheer,
Laughter echoes, far and near.

Humor at the Edge of Space

At the brink of endless night,
Witty thoughts take off in flight.
Comedic stardust fills the void,
Banter fuels the fun, enjoyed.

In the weightless, joy abounds,
Grinning faces with no bounds.
Shooting stars with laughter's gleam,
Beyond the void, we drift and dream.

Jovial Journeys

In a realm where giggles float,
And laughter's gravity can't be caught,
Jellybeans drift in a candy whirl,
As spacemen twirl in a sugary swirl.

Wormholes lead to a pie-filled space,
Where clowns juggle stars with a funny face,
Shooting stars are just puns in flight,
Bouncing jokes keep the mood so light.

Ethereal Antics

Balloons navigate the void with glee,
Chasing comets, utterly carefree,
A slapstick tumble from a floating chair,
Leaves giggles trailing in the cosmic air.

Each alien's laugh is a bubbling bloom,
As aliens dance in zero's room,
With cosmic cream pies as their delight,
This jolly chaos expands the night.

Cosmic Comedy

In starlit theaters with no ground,
Space jesters leap round and round,
With whispers of cheese from a moonlit shop,
They toss cosmic jokes that never stop.

A spaceship filled with rubber ducks,
In a game of tag with cosmic trucks,
Echoes of giggles bounce off the stars,
As punchlines orbit Venus and Mars.

Celestial Glee

In a nebula of ticklish delight,
Where the giggling meteors dance through the night,
Comedic comets whiz by with a grin,
Bringing joy to the space where we spin.

Zero-g somersaults, all in a row,
Wipeouts that send them all to and fro,
With each silly tumble, the heavens cheer,
For laughter, it seems, knows no frontier.

Galactic Foolery

In a spaceship full of snacks,
Clumsy astronauts trip on packs.
Floating cups spill cosmic tea,
Watch them laugh in weightless glee.

Stars twinkle with a cheeky grin,
Spacesuits wobble, oh, what a spin!
Zero G gives room to dance,
As they twirl in cosmic romance.

Comets zoom past, what a race,
Funky moves in endless space.
They play tag with little moons,
Singing silly, merry tunes.

Gravity? What a boring tale,
In this realm, we lightly sail.
With each giggle, we ignite,
Laughter echoes through the night.

Laughter Beyond Limits

Jokes float by like shooting stars,
Ticklish laughter, all the bars.
In this void, we toss and tease,
Cheeky quips drift on the breeze.

Asteroids join in for a laugh,
Making a joke out of their path.
With each chuckle, we defy,
The laws of physics, oh my my!

Cosmic clowns in orbits twirl,
Silly antics make us whirl.
Pluto jokes with Mars and Venus,
In this circus, ain't it genius?

In the silence, sounds erupt,
The vastness hugs us, it's corrupt.
But worry not, joy's always near,
In every giggle, there's no fear.

Ethereal Mirth

Floating high on silver beams,
Dreams collide with silly schemes.
Galaxies giggle, stars conspire,
With laughter fueling cosmic fire.

Nebulae blush in sparkly hues,
While cosmic jesters share their news.
Puns transcend through endless night,
In a ballet of pure delight.

Planets wobble, causing fuss,
As we ride this merry bus.
Light-years fly on giddy trails,
With each joke, the universe pales.

We bounce off nothing, where's the ground?
In this space, joy's truly found.
With every joke, we intertwine,
In the sweet void, so divine.

Serendipity in the Void

In empty space where we collide,
Silly bubbles of joy, we ride.
Gravity giggles, what a tease,
Drifting dreams on cosmic breeze.

Frolicking through the vast expanse,
Every star here loves to dance.
Glitches in time, we laugh aloud,
At the quirks that seem so proud.

Lunar llamas float on by,
With feathered hats, they touch the sky.
Each laugh a spark in endless black,
We'll make a joke and never look back.

With each twist of the stardust whirl,
We find the spark that makes us twirl.
In the universe, we're never lost,
For every chuckle, we pay the cost.

The Frivolity of Space

Floating past stars with a grin,
Astronauts chuckle, let the fun begin.
Wobbling in orbits, laughter in tow,
In this cosmic dance, silly thoughts flow.

Zero-G pranks with a whoopee cushion,
A galaxy giggles, sparks of elation.
Rocket fuel jokes that tickle the mind,
In the vastness, joy's never hard to find.

Celestial Brigade of Laughter

Beaming bright in the void they roam,
Against the backdrop, this is their home.
A comet's tail plays a cheeky game,
With humor that glimmers, never the same.

They juggle planets like oversized balls,
As meteors tumble and gravity stalls.
In every twist, a pun takes its flight,
In the cosmic circus, joy ignites the night.

Endlessly Amusing

An asteroid rolls with a giggly spin,
In the vacuum, silliness starts to win.
Light-years away, they share a delight,
Each supernova sparkles, a comedic light.

Through wormholes they tumble, in fits of glee,
No weight on their shoulders, wild and free.
Starships adorned with jokes to impart,
In the universe's laughter, they find their art.

Anti-Gravity Folly

With cosmic marbles, they race through the stars,
No finish line needed, just smiles and guitars.
Planets collide in a wacky dance,
As laughter erupts in this galactic trance.

A spacewalk of jokes, they drift in a line,
Dodging the sun with a punchline divine.
In this frivolous void, they spin and they fly,
With every chuckle, they lighten the sky.

Unbound Euphoria

Floating through the air with glee,
A rubber chicken flies by me.
Laughter echoes, deep and wide,
In this realm, we take a ride.

Juggling moons with silly flair,
Knocking comets, unaware.
Zero-grav and cheer collide,
Knock, knock jokes from the other side.

Gravity's pulling, but we're too light,
Cackling softly in the night.
Whirling like a cosmic dance,
In midair, we take our chance.

Here we spin with joyous grace,
Each tickle crafted in this space.
With giggles curling, we embrace,
A starry jam in endless chase.

Eclipsed Smiles

A solar panel wearing shades,
Distracts the stars in playful trades.
The moon complains, "It's just not fair!"
As laughter circles everywhere.

Galactic jokes like shooting stars,
Humor sprinkled 'round on Mars.
Wormholes twist in funny bends,
Where every journey never ends.

Cosmic pies are flying high,
Cream-filled orbs, oh my, oh my!
In a world where punchlines soar,
We find our joy, and then some more.

With every laugh, we start to sway,
The universe joins in the play.
Around the world, the chuckles roll,
A quirky game that fills the soul.

The Antigravity Comedy

Laughter bounces off the walls,
As everyone around me sprawls.
An upside-down, swing of jest,
In this space, we feel our best.

The punchlines land like drifting dust,
In zero maps, we simply trust.
With giggles ricocheting loud,
We form a merry, floating crowd.

Punching bags in orbital glee,
each hit sounds like a bumblebee.
Flying fish and clownish gnomes,
Create a world we call our own.

With every twist, our spirits sway,
Chasing clouds that laugh and play.
This cosmic stage, a surreal walk,
Where smiles rise and never fall.

Stardust Shenanigans

We launch from docks and spin around,
   Comets tumble, spinning sound.
  A rubber band in endless stretch,
   Signs of joy we always fetch.

   An alien sings a funny tune,
While planets twirl beneath the moon.
With sprinkles bright, we serve up fun,
 As laughter flies and jokes are spun.

  Floating pranks on solar sails,
  Tickling bits of cosmic trails.
  Glinting stars with silly grins,
 We ride the waves as humor wins.

With every twinkle, laughter grows,
  In this void, lighthearted flows.
 As stardust plays in gleeful arcs,
 We drift through nights that spark.

Jocular Celestial Bodies

Stars giggle, spinning in the void,
Planets trip on trails of asteroids.
Nebulas puff clouds of cosmic cheer,
While comets play tag, oh so near.

Asteroids sing with a raucous tune,
Bouncing through space like a zany cartoon.
Black holes yawn, with a riddle to share,
Pulling in laughter from everywhere.

Galaxies twist in a jolly dance,
Whirling and swirling in a graceful prance.
Cosmic clowns with gravity-free grace,
Tease the dark matter, partake in their race.

In this vast stage, the sun lobs a joke,
Light years giggle, neither can choke.
The Milky Way chuckles, a swirl of delight,
In a universe where humor takes flight.

Whimsical Wonders Above

In the night sky, chuckles abound,
Floating giggles from planets, unbound.
Moons pull the tides, a playful tease,
While meteor showers drop like confetti with ease.

Saturn wears rings, a costume so bright,
Juggling tiny moons in a slapstick light.
Uranus quips with a tilt so spry,
As stars wink secrets from a cosmic high.

Constellations dance in a comic spree,
Laughter echoes through infinity.
Gravity grabs, but the humor escapes,
As galaxies morph into silly shapes.

In this circus of orbs, laughter's the key,
A playful ballet in the deep, wild sea.
Stardust tickles the hearts that see,
Whimsical wonders, forever carefree.

Serenity in Space

Floating softly through the velvet night,
Stars whisper softly, oh what a sight.
Planets pose with a serene grace,
Yet tumblehead over heels in their place.

A calm asteroid, rocking to and fro,
Shares tales of giggles only it could know.
Silent orbits, a dance of peace,
Yet boisterous echoes help smiles increase.

Vacuum's hush seems to invite a grin,
The cosmos chuckles, with tickles within.
Quasars chuckle, a beam of bright fun,
While black holes refine their classic pun.

In this serene, yet joyous expanse,
Comets caper in a cosmic dance.
Stars hum lullabies, deceptively sweet,
While laughter is fleeting, a delightful treat.

Comedic Horizons

Across horizons, where laughter is born,
Planets frolic, like creatures reborn.
Shooting stars crack jokes on a whim,
While time loiters, addressing the grim.

Jovial Jupiter, with a grin so wide,
Shares its belly laughs on a cosmic ride.
Infinity winks, behind the veil,
As spaceships cruise on a joyful trail.

The universe beams, wrapped in delight,
As celestial beings dance through the night.
Cosmic puppets, in strings of pure light,
Pulling humor from the pockets of night.

Here, far from earthly stress and fight,
Galaxies giggle in shared delight.
With comedic horizons forever unspooled,
In this cosmic jest, we're endlessly fooled.

Cosmic Chuckles

Stars wink and dance in the air,
Galaxies spin without a care.
Whispers of comets tickle the night,
Floating in laughter, pure delight.

Asteroids giggle, dodging with glee,
While spacemen juggle zero-grav tea.
Nebulas puff like cotton candy,
Cosmic jokes, delightfully dandy.

Planets spin with a cheeky grin,
Rockets blast off, where to begin?
Each moment a chance to laugh and soar,
In this vast playground, we endlessly explore.

Dreaming Light

Waking up in a light-filled dream,
Lightyears away, all is a gleam.
Sleepy asteroids snore through the night,
While moons play hide and seek with delight.

Sirens of laughter sing soft in space,
Galactic giggles in a starry embrace.
Comets race, with humor in tow,
Ready for mischief, high and low.

In this whimsical ballet, we sway,
Stardust tickles and leads us astray.
Light beams twist in a playful dance,
Spinning us into a cosmic trance.

Gravity's Playful Echo

Without gravity, we bounce and sway,
Floating in joy, come join the play.
Echoes of laughter ripple and rise,
While black holes chuckle in darkened skies.

Meteor showers rain down tickles,
As astronauts bust out their silly giggles.
Planets juggle in a cosmic spree,
Funny faces in zero-G.

Falling stars wish for a good laugh,
Charting a course through a giggle graph.
Gravity's bounds can never contain,
Fun that echoes in a joyful refrain.

Laughter Lost in Space

Drifting slowly through space's quarry,
Where silence hides and echoes worry.
A spaceship soars with silly banter,
In the void, our jokes grow fancier.

Light flickers and shadows play games,
As floating laughter calls out names.
Galaxies whisper punchlines so wise,
Dancing fast in our starry skies.

With every trip, we float through mirth,
Finding joy in this cosmic girth.
Lost in laughter, we roam the night,
Chasing the stars, hearts ever light.

Joy Boundless

In a dance with the stars, we twirl so light,
Giggling amidst comets, oh what a sight.
Gravity's a prank, in this cosmic spree,
We bounce and we tumble, wild and free.

Bananas in space? Now that's a treat!
Floating through laughter, we can't be beat.
Our joy's a balloon, too big to pop,
In this vastness of fun, we'll never stop.

The Quintessence of Play

With wobbly cheese moons, we play catch above,
Juggling with asteroids, giggles we love.
Zero-suit pranks, oh what a delight,
Laughter's the fuel that ignites the night.

Each giggle a rocket, we soar without cares,
Tickling stars as we float through layers.
Cosmic confetti, it's raining with glee,
The essence of joy in this wild galaxy.

Laughs Across Lightyears

Warping through jokes, we skip and we glide,
Time's just a joke, lets laughter be our guide.
Who knew the cosmos could tickle so sweet?
With Milky Way puns, our hearts skip a beat.

Nebulae cheer while we chase shooting stars,
Riding a wave of hilarity's bars.
Distance is silly, we're just a short leap,
Laughs echo softly, through darkness so deep.

Zero-Gravity Joyride

Warm smiles in orbit, we float by delight,
Twisting through giggles, in the softest night.
Cosmic rollercoaster, a trip made of cheer,
Every twist and turn, brings us near.

Prancing past planets, we hoot and we holler,
Laughter's a spaceship, helping us boller.
Astro-clowns cavorting, gravity's no match,
In this buoyant frolic, there's always a catch.

The Bubbles of Delight.

In a vacuum, both light and sound,
Laughter bounces all around.
Bubbles float with giggling grace,
As we drift in this joyous space.

Tickling toes as we spin about,
Chasing squeaky toys, no doubt.
A silly dance with no floor to cling,
In weightless air, we laugh and sing.

Gravity's Whimsy

Upside down, I sip my tea,
A wobbly friend smiles back at me.
Teacups swirl in cosmic dance,
Every sip's a playful chance.

With a grin, I toss a spoon,
It twirls and glides, a merry tune.
Gravity's gone, but fun prevails,
In this madcap world of floating trails.

Floating Laughter Echoes

Echoes of giggles filled the air,
A cosmic comedy, beyond compare.
Juggling stars with silly smirks,
As joy in zero-gravity lurks.

A tumble here and a flip there,
We twirl through space without a care.
Counting how many moons we see,
Each one laughs along with glee.

Celestial Playgrounds

Rocket swings and comet slides,
We launch into laughter, where fun resides.
Galactic slides of playful glee,
In this vast space, we're wild and free.

Bouncing off planets, joyful cheers,
Tickled by stars, forgetting our fears.
A carousel made of nebulae,
Round and round, we spin and fly.

Orbital Lullabies

Floating dreams in space's grace,
Silly thoughts in zero place.
Stars are winking, shadows dance,
In this weightless, wacky trance.

Rocket ships with giggles sway,
Asteroids play hide and play.
Cosmic tunes in silent space,
Laughter echoes, fills the place.

Antigravity Giggles

Up above in the moon's embrace,
Frogs in suits do a funny race.
Jellybeans float, a sugar craze,
Gravity's lost in the laughing maze.

Balloons that drift and tickle toes,
Silly hats on moonlight clothes.
Puppies bouncing, tails in flight,
Guffaws unravel through the night.

Laughter Among the Stars

Stars are chefs with cosmic pies,
Whipped cream clouds and twinkling skies.
Astro-bunnies munching cheese,
Each giggle floats upon the breeze.

Dancing comets make a scene,
With sparkly hats and smiles keen.
Galactic games in playful twirls,
Unicorns spin with frothy swirls.

Cosmic Chuckles

Planets sing in joyful cheer,
Playful sounds for all to hear.
Orbits twirl as laughter flies,
In the vastness, joy defies.

Swirls of stardust, happy cries,
Celestial jesters paint the skies.
In this realm of pure delight,
Wit and whimsy unite so bright.

Jesting in the Cosmos

Galactic clowns float by,
With giggles that roam free.
Asteroids roll with laughter,
In this wild space comedy.

Stars wink with a knowing grin,
While comets chase their tails.
Laughter bounces off the moons,
As gravity ignores the fails.

Nebulas dance like crazy,
Painting colors on the void.
Each twist and turn is silly,
In this joy we can't avoid.

Here in the vast expanse,
Echos of chuckles chase.
What a cosmic fun-time prank,
In this outer space embrace.

Unfettered Delight

Zero-G bounces all around,
Silly flips and carefree spins.
Laughter leaves its weight behind,
As joy in orbit always wins.

Floating pies and jello jigs,
Navigating with a laugh.
Every drift a playful prank,
In this buoyant joyful path.

As we twirl like whirling dervishes,
The universe joins the cheer.
Each quirk in space adds to the fun,
Every chuckle's like a tear.

In stellar fields of goofy dreams,
Laughter rolls like shooting stars.
Joyful chaos fills the night,
As we play with cosmic jars.

Playful Paradoxes

An astronaut wears a jester's hat,
With space boots made of foam.
Witty quips float through the air,
In this lofty, floating home.

Even the planets join the act,
In a dance with zero grace.
They twist and giggle, spin in glee,
Creating a humorous space.

A black hole snickers softly,
As it swallows up the light.
While meteors tell dad jokes,
On this whimsical flight.

Here, the cosmos plays pretend,
In a theater without walls.
Laughter stretches beyond the stars,
In our weightless, merry halls.

Laughter in Orbit

Orbiting like a merry-go-round,
We spin through giggles and grins.
Funny planets play hide and seek,
As the interstellar fun begins.

Asteroids with silly faces,
Drift slowly past with flair.
Each collision brings a joke,
In this light, floating air.

Gravity's taken a vacation,
While humor breaks the mold.
With each upheaval of laughter,
A new cosmic tale unfolds.

Float on, my stellar friends,
With smiles that light the dark.
In this humor-laden sky,
Joy's the spark that leaves its mark.

Atmosphere of Amusement

In space so bright, we laugh and glide,
With zero weight, our giggles ride.
The stars all twinkle, a comic scene,
As we float high, like a silly dream.

The aliens chuckle, they join the fun,
With goofy smiles, they dance and run.
Galactic jokes fly like shooting stars,
In this joyland, we're all bizarre!

Bouncing laughter, the space like cream,
Our cosmic playground, a humorous dream.
Weightless wonders keep spirits light,
In bubbly bliss, we laugh all night.

So raise a toast with a fizzy drink,
In this merry void, we'll never sink.
Let the cosmos laugh till it's dizzy and bright,
In our joyous expanse, we'll dance with delight!

Orbiting Grins

Floating around like a feathered prank,
In a dance of giggles, we share our tank.
The planets wink, oh what a sight,
As we tumble and spin in pure delight.

With comet tails trailing silly roars,
We race through space, dodging cosmic chores.
The universe shrieks with glee and fun,
While we sip stardust under a laughing sun.

Rockets wheeze with a comedic twist,
In this orbit, can anyone resist?
Whirling emotions in the vacuum reside,
As humor propels us through the cosmic tide.

Stars are our stage, with laughter to share,
Gliding through voids without a care.
In the humor of chaos, we find our groove,
Bouncing forever in this playful move!

Elysium of Elation

Sprinkled joy from the Milky Way,
We giggle and twirl, in endless play.
With quarks and quirks, our laughter expands,
Creating smiles across all lands.

In this blissful realm where all can float,
Improbable pranks are the best antidote.
Galactic whirls spin absurdity right,
As we twinkle our toes in the cosmic light.

The moons are jesters, the comets jest,
In this arena, we're truly blessed.
With every bounce, our spirits soar,
In a carousel of joy, we always want more.

Shooting laughter like starlit rays,
Celebrating glee in absurd ways.
Here in our haven, it's laughter we seek,
In this zero-G jest, we find our peak!

Cosmic Curiosities

Wacky droids twirl with gleeful sounds,
In this boundless space, where humor abounds.
Floating past planets on squishy beans,
We tickle stardust and dance on scenes.

Galaxies giggle, what a sight to behold,
With each quirk and twist, our stories unfold.
The laughter echoes through nebulous lanes,
In a zany cycle where everyone gains.

Cosmic clowning on gravity's flight,
Our antics whirl, both day and night.
With wobbly jesters and comical stars,
We'll frolic together, no matter how far.

In our boundless circus, we'll twirl and cheer,
As merriment dances, there's nothing to fear.
So buckle up tight for this laughing spree,
In the great cosmic quest, forever carefree!

Gravity's Laughter

In the void, we float and glide,
With laughter echoing far and wide.
A pancake flip, we twist and spin,
In zero-G, let the silliness begin.

Chasing socks, a cosmic dance,
Who knew space could have such a chance?
We giggle as we tumble high,
No gravity here, just a joyful sigh.

The stars wink down, they know our game,
In this vast dome, we're all the same.
A comet's tail becomes our slide,
With every bounce, we're filled with pride.

Floating cakes and fizzy streams,
As we chase our wildest dreams.
In this realm of endless jest,
Life's a party; we're forever blessed.

Celestial Nonsense

Up in space, what a sight,
Jellybeans zoom left and right.
A cat in a hat, what a surprise,
When it sings, the sun starts to rise.

Galactic giggles and silly cheers,
As we bounce off the moon without fears.
A rubber chicken with no bounds,
In the cosmos, it happily bounds.

Socks start dancing, shoes in tow,
In this dimension, who needs a show?
We juggle stars, we toss and roll,
In this orbit, we've found our soul.

Floating visions, a cosmic fair,
Spinning tales in the brisk air.
With each laugh, we craft our fate,
Celestial nonsense – isn't it great?

Cosmic Whimsy

In the sky where whimsy spins,
Laughing comets, where fun begins.
We ride on waves of laughter's song,
In this dance, we cannot go wrong.

A moonbeam's grin, a winking star,
Floating near and yet so far.
Bubblegum planets, sweet and bright,
Twirl with joy in the velvet night.

Dancing robots, what a sight,
As they glide in sheer delight.
With every twirl, we tease the sun,
Cosmic whimsy - oh, what fun!

Banana boats on glitter streams,
Where nothing's ever as it seems.
A cosmos filled with playful sparks,
In this realm, we leave our marks.

Weightless Revelry

Bouncing softly, we glide through air,
Weightless revelry, beyond compare.
A twirling dance on starlit floors,
We toast to dreams and cosmic tours.

Asteroids fly, we toss and catch,
In laughter's sphere, all dreams match.
Giggles soar, like bubbles they rise,
As we witness wondrous skies.

A llama floats with a goofy smile,
Sharing joy across the mile.
With every chuckle, we drift and sway,
In this endless game we play.

Slapping high-fives with a meteor's tail,
Riding comets without fail.
Together we shine in this endless spree,
In weightless revelry, just you and me.

Cheerful Frontiers

Bouncing through the cosmic sea,
With giggles in our zero suits,
Stars wink and tease the gravity,
While we spin in orbit loops.

Tickles from the starlit haze,
As planets rotate with a laugh,
We juggle meteors in rays,
Crafting joy from each mishap.

Floating in the moons' embrace,
Silly faces, pure delight,
Shooting stars we try to chase,
In this vast, hilarious flight.

A comet's tail like whipped cream,
We dive into its frosty swirl,
Every swirl's a giddy dream,
In this boundless, merry whirl.

Zero-Gravity Grins

In a bubble, smiles extend,
Ballooning dreams that never end,
Galaxies giggle, stars ignite,
As laughter takes us through the night.

We flip and flop, we float and glide,
Embracing every cosmic ride,
With every bump, we crack a joke,
'Til even Saturn's rings now smoke.

Silly songs in stellar tunes,
Echo through the bright draped moons,
We spin each tale in vibrant hues,
In zero-g, where whimsy brews.

Planet's pranks around us whirl,
As space-time bends in frosty twirl,
Our joyful hearts, in tune and dance,
In a realm of carefree chance.

Joyride Among Comets

Slip and slide through asteroid fields,
Where laughter's echo brightly yields,
Comets with a flair for fun,
Dancing like a rascally sun.

Zero-grav's our playground sweet,
A waltz with space, a bouncing beat,
Twisting galaxies share a grin,
As we juggle time and spin.

Rocket trails leave trails of joy,
Planets bounce like a playful toy,
With every giggle, new worlds wake,
In this vast void, we dance and shake.

A cartwheel through the giggling stars,
Gifts of mirth wrapped in moonbeams are,
On this cosmic road, we sail,
Sailing on laughter, a joyful trail.

Laughter's Quantum Dance

In a space where fun collides,
We float and twirl with cosmic tides,
Every atom's got a grin,
As joy and mischief dance within.

Through neutron stars and supernovae,
Our spirits play, come what may,
With each tickle of the breeze,
Quarks do wobbly, funny freeze.

We leap through loops of time and space,
Sharing giggles with a stellar face,
What a sight, a playful sway,
Where humor lights the cosmic way.

A laughter wave, so easy flows,
Spreading joy wherever it goes,
In this realm of mighty jest,
We spin forever, feeling blessed.

Comedic Celestial Drift

Floating through the void with glee,
A cosmic dance, just you and me.
We spin like tops, no care at all,
No gravity here, we're bound to fall.

Asteroids chuckle, stars delight,
While we juggle moons, what a sight!
In zero-grav, there's no mistake,
We laugh so hard, we make it quake.

Wobbling through hands and feet,
A slapstick show, oh what a feat!
A comet sweeps, we take a dive,
The punchline lands, we feel alive.

Twirling quickly, we lose our snack,
Floating popcorn, oh what a knack!
In this vast space, we find our jest,
As laughter echoes, it feels the best.

Airborne Antics

Up in the sky, where giggles soar,
We leap with joy, who could want more?
Bouncing off walls in a merry spree,
Floating wildly, just you and me.

Cosmic chuckles pop like toast,
A funny face, we laugh the most.
With every turn, the stars will grin,
As our silly dances begin to spin.

With each new flip, the laughter grows,
We trip on stardust—how it flows!
Zero-G tickles, our giggles ring,
In this wild space, we can't stop swinging.

Lunar slides and stellar swings,
We'll board the laughs on laughter's wings.
Floating by in pure delight,
Gravity's joke, we hold on tight.

Space-Suspended Smiles

In a realm where silliness abounds,
We mix up laughter with cosmic sounds.
Floating high, our joy takes flight,
No bounds to pull us from our height.

Planets wink with mirthful cheer,
As we tumble, giggle, and reappear.
Our laughter shakes the stardust near,
In this orbit, nothing to fear.

A whimsical ride on a shooting star,
We navigate this chaos bizarre.
With each new roll, we jest and tease,
Our smiles float like soft summer breeze.

Hitching rides on solar rays,
In twists and turns, our spirits blaze.
No gravity holds us, just our jest,
In this vast expanse, we feel blessed.

Giddy Gravity

In the stillness of space, we're up to pranks,
Zero gravity? Let's fill the tanks!
Hovering high, we giggle and sway,
As starlight gleams, we dance and play.

Spacesuits tight, but laughter's loose,
Letting go of all that's obtuse.
Sliding on beams with a youthful cheer,
In this grand vacuum, we lose all fear.

Flip and flop with cosmic grace,
Giggles abound in this wondrous place.
A spacefarer's jest at the edge of night,
In this orbit, everything feels right.

With joy we twirl, it's a merry ride,
In this boundless void, where dreams confide.
A comedy act that never ends,
With laughter shining, as our new trend.

The Dance of Floating Dreams

In a realm where giggles soar,
Dancing on clouds, who could ask for more?
Twisting and turning, so merry and light,
We waltz through the cosmos, what a delight!

Waving goodbye to the pull of the ground,
In this joke-studded sky, joy knows no bound.
With each silly shuffle, we rise and we twirl,
Creating a whirl of laughter and pearl.

Balloons float by in colors so bright,
They giggle and jiggle, a wondrous sight.
Caught in a spiral of joy and of jest,
Our dreams drift along, unencumbered, the best!

As meteors wink and comets go zoom,
We laugh at the dark, create our own bloom.
In a world of pure whimsy, no reason to fret,
The dance of our dreams is one we won't forget.

Gravity's Paradox

Oh, silly forces, you've lost your might,
We bounce off the walls, what a bizarre flight!
With chuckles erupting, we glide and we roll,
In this loopy domain, we've found our true role.

Falling upwards, it tickles our souls,
Jokes on the planets, we're taking control.
Each flip brings a giggle, oh what a tease,
Playing with physics, oh how we please!

Bananas float by, wearing hats made of cheese,
Shooting stars giggle, putting us at ease.
Caught in a spiral of humor and play,
In this paradox realm, let's dance the whole day!

From one side to another, we bounce with delight,
Twirling in zero-g, life feels so right.
With laughter as fuel, and joy as our guide,
We'll spin through the cosmos, let fun be our ride!

Laughter Among the Stars

In the vastness of space, where giggles resound,
We're tickled by stardust that swirls all around.
With echoes of laughter, we float hand in hand,
Creating a party, celestial and grand.

Asteroids roll by, dressed up like a clown,
While planets spin tales, upside down, upside down.
Each nova bursts forth with a puff full of glee,
A cosmic shin-dig, come join in the spree!

Stars wink like children, oh, what a sight,
They chuckle and dance through the beautiful night.
Galactic confetti falls down like a dream,
In this swirling laughter, we're all part of the team.

Enjoying the ride from the Earth to the moon,
As our spirits take flight, like a merry cartoon.
With smiles as our guide, through the cosmos we roam,
In laughter and light, we've created our home!

Zero-Gravity Giggles

Weightless we wander, in joy we are found,
Frolicking freely, no worries around.
With each comical bounce, we're bursting with cheer,
In a world turned upside down, nothing's to fear.

Floating like feathers in a ticklish breeze,
We burst into laughter with effortless ease.
Joking with moons, spinning tales with a flare,
In this whimsical ballet, no frowning to share.

Oh, how the comets shimmer with glee,
As we tumble and spin, oh so merrily.
With every soft squeal, we create a new plot,
In this merry-go-space, we give it all we've got!

So let's twirl and whirl, in this timeless delight,
Where laughter's our beacon, guiding us right.
In zero-g bliss, we're forever entwined,
In a universe chuckling, we leave cares behind!

Weightless Whimsy

In a world where laughter floats free,
Giggles drift like stars in spree.
Tickles chase all worries and care,
Joy swirls around in midair.

Balloons bounce off the cosmic floor,
Jokes take flight, who could ask for more?
Gravity's pranks make us spin and twirl,
Each chuckle a loop in this merry whirl.

Bananas glide, a slippery race,
While we drift with a grin on each face.
Orbiting punchlines, so silly and bright,
We'll laugh till we reach the next night.

A comet of giggles, a meteor of cheer,
Weightless whimsy is always near.
In this endless vault, we play and we jest,
Floating through fun, we are truly blessed.

The Dance of Zero Gravity

Twirl through the void with a skip and a spin,
Floating through joy is how we begin.
With each little bounce, we toss cares away,
And dance like the stars to the rhythm of play.

A partner in laughter, come twirl up with me,
We'll glide through the cosmos so carelessly.
Feet barely touching the colorful ground,
While giggles and smiles are the only sound.

Marshmallow moonsbeam down like delight,
Pairing up shadows in the soft, gentle light.
We lose track of time as we swirl and we sway,
In a waltz of the silly, we drift and we play.

In this weightless ballroom, let joy take its cue,
The universe chuckles, a lively debut.
So raise your hands high, let your spirit be free,
In the dance of the stars, it's just you and me.

Joy in the Void

In the vastness where silence sings,
Float along with whimsical things.
Giggling stars tickle my nose,
As laughter in vacuum eternally flows.

Bounce off bright asteroids, spin with the light,
Joy finds a way in the heart of the night.
Whispers of chuckles drift soft through the air,
In this void of delight, worries vanish with flair.

A parade of pinwheels and colorful kites,
Lead us through laughter in our gravity flights.
With every small poke of our jester's delight,
The universe twinkles, our joy's taking flight.

So come grab a comet, let's fly for a while,
Dancing in nothing, adventures compile.
With a wink and a grin, the cosmos a-shimmer,
In the heart of the void, our spirits grow dimmer.

Stellar Shenanigans

Hold on tight to the wobbly, bright cheer,
As we zoom past the stars with naught but a sneer.
Shooting for giggles, we aim for the moon,
Space is our playground, let's linger till noon.

Alien giggles and shenanigans soar,
As comets confetti all float to the floor.
With each mishap a laugh, a stumble, a roll,
This cosmic caper ignites every soul.

Planets will chuckle and echo our fun,
As we cartwheel through patterns of light from the sun.
In this weightless wonder, the world is a jest,
Wit marks the sky in the levity fest.

Let's bounce on the rings of a dazzling thing,
And join in the laughter that starlight can bring.
In a cosmos of chaos, we find our sweet bliss,
A stellar adventure, we'll giggle and hiss.

Serendipitous Smirks

In a twist of fate, we float around,
Bouncing off walls, we dance, unbound.
With every twist, a laugh erupts,
As gravity's grace hilariously disrupts.

Cups of coffee drift in the air,
With sips that vanish, we just don't care.
Umbrella hats in a cosmic breeze,
We're fashion icons in space, oh please!

Wormhole wind-up toys spin with glee,
Chasing stardust, just you and me.
Giggles echo in this endless flight,
As time ticks funny, day turns to night.

What's lost is found in a blink so fast,
A game of tag, the die is cast.
Serendipitous smirks abound in space,
In this carefree, floaty, laughter chase.

The Joyride of Existence

Riding comets on this joyride sweet,
Floating backwards, what a funny feat!
Stars poke fun, twinkling bright,
Turning our missteps into pure delight.

Galactic slides and cosmic swings,
In zero-G, we invent new things.
Slips and trips on nebula's edge,
Laughter erupts as we make our pledge.

Mirthful whispers of the solar breeze,
Wishing on shooting stars with ease.
Out here, the silly rules still apply,
With ticklish meteors passing by.

The joyride thickens, oh what a scene,
We're the stars, the bright and the keen.
In this zany dance, we spin and twirl,
Existence is funny, let the laughter unfurl.

Spacebound Revelry

Floating high in laughter's embrace,
Gravity's got nothing on our race.
With every giggle, we defy the grind,
In this spacebound revelry, joy's our find.

Silly hats and quirky shoes,
In the cosmos, there's no room to lose.
Asteroids chuckle at our delight,
As we twirl, wobble, and dance through the night.

Pluto's our DJ, spinning tunes so bright,
In the silence, our laughter takes flight.
Galactic bubbles float and collide,
In a whimsical party, come join the ride!

With cosmic confetti raining down,
We wear the universe like a crown.
Spacebound revelry, so wild and free,
In this boundless joy, it's just you and me.

A Nebulous Laughter

In a fog of giggles, we float around,
Nebulas bloom with a whimsical sound.
Comedic antics dance through the air,
In this soft haze, we banish despair.

Spinning planets trade winks and grins,
As stars share snickers, everyone wins.
Clouds of laughter, thick like cream,
In this cosmic space, we share a dream.

Here, time's a joke that tickles the mind,
In echoes of joy, our hearts unwind.
The universe chuckles in playful cheer,
A nebulous laughter, forever near.

With each new bounce, in this void we thrive,
Sailing through space, oh, how we're alive!
In giggling whirlwinds, we orbit and sway,
A myriad of fun in our own ballet.

A Universe of Chuckles

Galaxies giggle, spinning so bright,
Stars wear glasses, flip-flops in flight.
Asteroids chuckle, rolling with glee,
Cosmic jokes whispered from tree to tree.

Silly black holes, they pull without care,
Swallowing laughter, they just love to share.
Comets are jokers with tails that delight,
They zip past with punchlines, what a sight!

Nebula's Nonsense

In a cloud of colors, chaos has fun,
Planets are pranks from the moon to the sun.
Little green aliens dance in a ring,
They jive to the rhythm of cosmic zing.

Each supernova erupts with a cheer,
Spreading the giggles all over the sphere.
Nebulae twirl in a whimsical waltz,
Making mischief with no hint of faults.

Celestial Capers

Floating in space, a cat on a beam,
Chasing a comet, living the dream.
Planets wear hats, oh what a sight,
Saturn's ringmaster manages the night.

Meteor showers, a confetti parade,
Dancing with laughter, never afraid.
Stars tell tall tales on their glowing stage,
While the universe giggles, it just won't age.

Utopian Float

In this realm of whimsy, all float and sway,
Cosmic giggles echo all night and day.
Planets play tag, a raucous delight,
While moons crack jokes, oh what a sight!

In this bucolic void, fun takes the lead,
Starry-eyed mischief, a buoyant creed.
Comets toss pies, while the suns all cheer,
In this zero-gravity, laughter draws near.

Stars with a Smile

Twinkling lights in cosmic dance,
Winking bright, they take a chance.
Giggles float on solar winds,
As planets spin, their laughter grins.

Jupiter jokes, and Saturn sighs,
In swirling skirts, the comet flies.
A cosmic party, quite the show,
With shooting stars in joyful tow.

Mars tells tales of greenish past,
While Venus chuckles, sharing laughs.
Galaxies with thriving wit,
Making time a playful skit.

So on this night, look up with glee,
For in the stars, pure mirth we see.
In universe's wild embrace,
Laughter lives in outer space.

Sliding Through the Cosmos

Slipping past on beams of light,
Riding waves of endless night.
Gravity grabs, but doesn't hold,
With jests and jives, we break the mold.

Asteroids skate with playful grace,
While comets grin in cosmic race.
Pulsars beep with rhythmic cheer,
As rockets bounce away from fear.

Nebulas swirl in colors bright,
Their laughter echoes through the night.
In space's arms, we glide and spin,
With grinning stars, let fun begin!

Through constellations, we take flight,
With playful spirits, hearts alight.
On this grand ride, we can't resist,
The humor found in every twist.

Amusing Angels

Angels float in fluffy clouds,
Trading jokes in gleeful crowds.
Their wings a-flutter, laughter sings,
As they toss around the silly things.

One tells tales of lands afar,
While next to him, a twinkling star.
They chuckle at the moon's old face,
In a heavenly, joyous space.

With halos high and spirits bold,
They dance in circles, brave and bold.
From the highest peaks, humor showers,
Blessing all with giggling powers.

As they glide through skies so wide,
Their funny sparks can never hide.
In every laugh, a soulful blend,
Of joy that knows no end.

Dreaming in Anti-Gravity

Floating dreams in weightless air,
We tumble, twirl, without a care.
Giggles burst like stars' delight,
In the stillness of the night.

Each thought a bubble, soaring high,
Tickling thoughts as they float by.
In playful pause, we drift and sway,
In a cosmic game, we choose to play.

With every spin, our worries fade,
In a whirl of joy, we serenade.
The universe hums a funny tune,
As we dance beneath a laughing moon.

So drift with dreams, both bright and free,
Embrace the whimsy, let it be.
In gravity's absence, laughter grows,
In an endless play, where humor flows.

Heavenly Hilarity

In the vastness, laughter flies,
Spinning like a comet's sigh.
Galactic pranks, a cosmic tease,
Float through space with utmost ease.

Alien jokes in zero-grav,
Falling up, we laugh and wave.
Wobbling giggles, silly spins,
Gravity? Who needs those sins?

Rocket-fueled jests collide,
Bouncing off the stars with pride.
Cosmic banter fills the void,
Where seriousness is destroyed.

Orbiting whimsies, endless cheer,
Tickling moons that persevere.
In this realm, fun has no end,
A starry chuckle, time to blend.

Fractured Reality of Fun

In this realm of joy absurd,
Floating thoughts like fluffy birds.
Zero-grav, where truth takes flight,
Bouncing joy from day to night.

Cartwheels on the Milky Way,
Twinkling stars in disarray.
Rockets soar, and giggles roar,
Each punchline knocks down the door.

Reality wobbles, laughs grow loud,
Expecting sense, the cosmos wowed.
Fractured pieces, yet we thrive,
With every jest, we feel alive.

Laughter's echo fills the space,
Gravity? Just a silly race.
Floating whimsies, cosmic dance,
In this jest, we too advance.

Amusing in Abeyance

Time suspended, joy prevails,
Floating giggles, cosmic trails.
In the quiet of the void,
Silly thoughts, never cloyed.

Astral puns in lazy spins,
Weightless laughter, where it begins.
Suspended joy, a funny gleam,
Drifting softly in a dream.

Twinkling stars share jokes untold,
As we float, we're never old.
In this ballet of mirthful jest,
Each cosmic moment is the best.

Orbiting humor, floats in air,
In this space, we have no care.
Whimsical wonders gently sway,
Abeyance blooms in every way.

Starlit Joyride

With every twist, the cosmos grins,
Galactic glee on stellar skins.
Riding comets, laughter bright,
Joy abounds in the starry night.

Hitch a ride on a shining trail,
Floating freely, we'll set sail.
Gravity lost, we spin and sway,
In this mirthful, weightless play.

Whimsical flights in deep space cheer,
Echoes of joy, crystal clear.
Galactic giggles fly like kite,
In the universe's funny light.

Around the sun, we twist and turn,
For cosmic laughs, we brightly yearn.
A starlit jaunt, where fun won't cease,
In this joyride, there's only peace.

Floating Follies

In a ship made of cheese, we drift and sway,
Cheddar comets lead us astray.
Galactic giggles around us spin,
As we tumble through space, let the fun begin!

With zero G, our snacks take flight,
Popcorn kernels dance in the light.
Astronauts bounce with a gleeful cheer,
Floating with laughter, nothing to fear!

Wobbling weights in the cosmic spree,
A jelly jar floats, and oh, what glee!
We sail on a whim in this vast delight,
Chasing moon pies in a meteorite!

Stars play tricks, they tease and wink,
While zero gravity gives us time to think.
A cosmic punchline, a mischief grand,
In the universe's joy, we make our stand.

Celestial Banter

In the quiet depths of the starry night,
Space squirrels chatter in glorious flight.
They juggle the moons, what a comical sight,
While we laugh and cheer in celestial delight!

Bounce like bubbles in a zero-grav world,
To cosmic rifts and giggles, we're hurled.
Planets parade in a whimsical line,
As we join in the folly, sipping starlit wine!

Gravity's gone, so we roll and spin,
Make duck-faced selfies with a cheese grin.
Asteroids chuckle, as we flip by,
In this cosmic circus, we reach for the sky!

Voices of nebulae whisper our tune,
While we boogie with quasars 'neath a silvery moon.
Under the light of a billion bright laughs,
Tripping through stardust, we've found our paths.

Laughing with the Cosmos

Galaxies giggle in a limitless space,
While we wobble 'round in an interstellar race.
Comets with winks swoosh through the air,
In this joke of a journey, we haven't a care!

Shooting stars tickle our shrieking delight,
As doughnuts float past in the velvety night.
With laughter as fuel, we soar and we glide,
On this merry adventure, we bumble with pride!

Sipping starlight from a cosmic cup,
Frolicking freely, can't get enough.
The universe chuckles, its humor so vast,
In this dance of the cosmos, we're having a blast!

Orbiting joy with a trampoline bounce,
Every leap's a joke, can you hear the pounce?
Together we spin in this heavenly fest,
Forever we'll laugh 'til we've reached our zest!

The Joy of Astral Absurdity

In a swirl of confetti, we float on a beam,
Jellybeans orbit in a sweet, silly dream.
Gravity's nonsense, a whimsical play,
As we giggle through stars, come join in our fray!

A dance of the planets, they twist and they twirl,
With laughter erupting, we're ready to whirl.
Bouncing on quarks, a frolicsome fate,
In this giddy expanse, we exuberantly skate!

Floating on giggles, we sip cosmic tea,
While black holes croon in hilarious glee.
A nebula's wink, oh, what a jest,
In the grand scheme of fun, we've been truly blessed!

So come, take a ride on this laughter spree,
In a universe brimming with joyous decree.
Together we'll tumble, forever we'll soar,
In the realm of the strange, there's always much more!

Orbital Ridiculousness

Floating in the cosmic spice,
A rubber chicken rolls like dice.
Aliens join in with a dance,
Defying gravity's fine prance.

Space clowns juggle stars so bright,
Tickle a comet, what a sight!
Galactic giggles whirl around,
In this absurd playground found.

Asteroids, they slip and slide,
With cosmic pies, oh what a ride!
Laughter echoes through the void,
Both joyful and slightly paranoid.

Astro-bunnies bounce with glee,
In zero-G, they're wild and free.
Chaos reigns, without a care,
In this world of harebrained flair.

Silhouettes of Silliness

Worms in space are quite a sight,
They twist and turn, what pure delight!
Dancing shadows drift and sway,
In cosmic hues, they play all day.

Banana rockets zoom on by,
With giggles that reach up to the sky.
Jupiter's moons wear silly hats,
While Saturn's rings play games with cats.

A cosmic pie fight's breaking out,
Galactic cream, there's no doubt!
As laughter starts to fill the space,
A pancake lands – what a face!

Light years away, fun seems so near,
In this ballet of joyful cheer.
Each moment twists in pure delight,
In starry nights that feel so right.

Elysium in the Atmosphere

In fluffy clouds of giggle gas,
Space cows moo as they float past.
Wobbly rainbows lead the way,
To where the silly creatures play.

A peanut spaceship zooms about,
With sassy pilots full of clout.
They sing a tune, both bright and loud,
In this absurd celestial crowd.

Shooting stars spin like tops,
While starfish do some lively hops.
In the ether, they take a chance,
For cosmic fun is quite a dance!

With every twist, a giggle pops,
As zero-G just never stops.
Caught in the whimsy of the night,
In this limitless flight of light.

Comedic Curiosities of the Cosmos

Pluto wears a polka-dot tie,
While Venus flirts and winks an eye.
Asteroids take a silly bow,
A comedy club just for the cow.

Martian marshmallows swirl and float,
While comets play the gagging goat.
With black holes cracking up in glee,
In this universe where we're all free.

Quasars giggle in their glow,
As space critters steal the show.
From lunar cucumbers' crazy flips,
To stellar soup with fishy sips.

Planets spin in a merry whirl,
As space-time bends with a twirly twirl.
In this wacky cosmic fest,
Every jest is truly the best.

Humor in the Heliopause

A comet tripped on cosmic light,
Its tail flew off in sheer delight.
Stars giggled in their endless dance,
While asteroids joined in at a chance.

Space dust sneezed with a funny sound,
While laughing black holes spun 'round.
Jupiter played tag with a moon,
And Saturn tossed rings like a balloon.

Galaxies chuckled, swirling wide,
As planets spun in a goofy ride.
Nebulae painted smiles in space,
In this vast void, we find our place.

A supernova burst with flair,
Leaving echoes of laughter in the air.
Amongst the cosmos, laughter grows,
In the void where the humor flows.

Cosmic Revelations of Fun

In the depths of the dark unknown,
Stars whisper secrets, rarely shown.
A blob of gas with a grin so sly,
Winks at comets that zoom on by.

Mars threw a party, a space-age bash,
With meteors dancing and planets that crash.
Asteroids cracking up in their flight,
As laughter echoed through the endless night.

Quasars giggle in a furious beam,
While black holes play hide-and-seek in a dream.
Lightyears away, a joke's on repeat,
As space-time folds under fun's upbeat.

Shockwaves giggle, a cosmic delight,
As galaxies twinkle in the quiet night.
In this universe of laughter's embrace,
Every moment a jest, a comical race.

Orbiting Smiles

Planets giggle with every spin,
While gravity dances and wears a grin.
A rogue asteroid with a silly hat,
Goes whizzing by, just imagine that!

Saturn's rings spin tales of cheer,
While Pluto jokes, "I'm still here!"
The Sun makes faces, oh what a sight,
As solar flares flicker with delight.

Nebulas puff like cotton candy,
As cosmic clowns juggle, oh so handy.
Each twinkle in the night sky glows,
With a punchline only the stardust knows.

In this swirling dance of joy divine,
We orbit smiles, drinking starry wine.
With laughter floating through the vast expanse,
Every star winks in a cosmic dance.

Gravitationally Unbound Glee

In a rocket of dreams, we drift and sway,
While giggles from Earth float far away.
The cosmos tickles with starlight beams,
As we ride the laughter of moonlit dreams.

Cosmic balloons in the darkest skies,
Bouncing around like playful spies.
With comets that tease and planets that squeak,
In zero gravity, the fun's unique.

Starship shenanigans, let's take a flight,
Where jokes are heavier than the darkest night.
Galactic giggles echo loud and clear,
In this vast universe, humor is near.

Dancing with joy, unbound by the pull,
We float in the glee, hearts ever full.
A universe woven with laughter's thread,
In this cosmic joke, let's all be led.

www.ingramcontent.com/pod-product-compliance
Lightning Source LLC
Chambersburg PA
CBHW051655160426
43209CB00004B/903